PENGUIN BOOKS

CLAY. WHEREABOUTS UNKNOWN

Craig Raine was born in 1944 and educated at Exeter College, Oxford. He became editor of *Quarto* in 1979 and was subsequently Poetry Editor at Faber from 1981 to 1991. He is now Fellow in English at New College, Oxford. His books of poetry are *The Onion, Memory* (1978), *A Martian Sends a Postcard Home* (1979) and *Rich* (1984). His libretto for Nigel Osborne's opera *The Electrification of the Soviet Union* was published in 1986. In 1988 *The Prophetic Book* was published in a limited edition by Correspondance des Arts, Łódź. His verse drama, *'1953'*, appeared in 1990 and his collection of literary essays, *Haydn and the Valve Trumpet*, in the same year. He is also the editor of *A Choice of Kipling's Prose* (1987) and *Rudyard Kipling: Selected Poetry* (Penguin, 1993). His epic poem, *History: The Home Movie* (Penguin, 1994), focuses on two families, the Pasternaks and the Raines, and is a unique history of twentieth-century Europe.

Craig Raine lives in Oxford with his wife, Ann Pasternak Slater, and their four children.

Clay. Whereabouts Unknown

Craig Raine

PENGUIN BOOKS

PENGUIN BOOKS

Published by the Penguin Group
Penguin Books Ltd, 27 Wrights Lane, London w8 5TZ, England
Penguin Books USA Inc., 375 Hudson Street, New York, New York 10014, USA
Penguin Books Australia Ltd, Ringwood, Victoria, Australia
Penguin Books Canada Ltd, 10 Alcorn Avenue, Toronto, Ontario, Canada M4V 3B2
Penguin Books (NZ) Ltd, 182–190 Wairau Road, Auckland 10, New Zealand

Penguin Books Ltd, Registered Offices: Harmondsworth, Middlesex, England

First published 1996
1 3 5 7 9 10 8 6 4 2

Typeset in 11/14.5 pt Monotype Janson
Typeset by Datix International Limited, Bungay, Suffolk
Printed in England by Clays Ltd, St Ives plc

Contents

THE PROPHETIC BOOK

THE PROPHETIC BOOK

1 *The Prophetic Book*

I will grant you the world
that is taken for granted:
the turban in a tangerine,
a snooker table, say,
with six suspensory bandages,
the lemon squeezer
in the men's urinal.

You will need to know
the names of stone:
Taynton, Clipsham, Anstrude, Besace,
Headington, Wheatley, Perou,
and then Savonnières Courteraie
which is quarried at Meuse.
Sweet shades of chamois leather.

The passionate kiss
of sellotape, a sofa
with its four cedillas,
the ripple of a running track,
pincushion harbours, starfish
strong as a tongue
will pleasure you.

Will pleasure you as much
as the sight of a steam-roller
seen as a scarab beetle,
or a beach as a ballroom
dancing with steps,
or a bather testing the sea
like a ballerina.

I will bring you the beauty of facts:
Southdown, Dalesbred, Dartmoor,
Derbyshire Gritstone, Bluefaced Leicester,
Herdwick, Hill Radnor, Devon Longwool,
Beulah Speckled-Face, Oxford Down,
Welsh Mountain, North Country Cheviot,
do not exhaust the names of our sheep.

There is so much to celebrate:
the fine rain making midges
on a pool, the appalled moon,
and the crescent moon at morning
which fades like fat
in a frying pan, the frail
unfocused greens of spring.

You will see the pelting rain
of string in Kentish hopfields
when the weather is clear,
enjoy the sound of squeaky shoes
when doves are beating overhead,
find out flamingoes
with polio legs, elephants

with laddered trunks.
Bounty and boon: the cracked light
in a goose's quill, like frozen vodka;
a hunter's mane plaited
into peonies; swallows
in their evening dress
flicker and swoon like Fred Astaire.

There are tiddlywinks
of light in the summer woods.
Play with them. The ironing board
has permanent lumbago. Pity it.
Pity the man on his motor bike
stamping his foot
and roaring with temper.

Fly in aeroplanes and see
the speedboat's shooting star
like someone striking a match,
the car-park's pharmacy of ampoules,
the reef-knot on a motorway,
the marquetry of fields,
a golf course appliquéd with bunkers.

I will pledge you what is here:
a thousand kinds of bread,
each with a shape and name,
happiness and its haemorrhage,
the homesick hardware store
which can only say home,
Goethe and the gift of death.

Maze of entrails. Solid heart.
Drinker of urine. Channel swimmer
with tiny goggles of flesh.
Penis threaded like a grub
or folded for a clitoris.
Anus plugged with liquorice.
Endive and coral bronchial tree.

Overlapping skull-plates.
Mollusc and master yogi,
standing on your head
with ankles crossed,
your horses are waiting
by the fringe of the weir,
cleft like broad beans with black.

Your train is leaving the station
like a labrador scratching at fleas.
The ticket collector
stands in confetti.
I give you this prophetic book,
this sampler of life
which will take you a lifetime to read.

A Polish midwife was assisting at my birth.
And I gave birth to a beautiful girl.
There on the stones. In my own filth.
No soap. No cotton wool. Without hot water.

I went to my cot. No mattress, just a cover.
And in the morning, Mengele.
My breasts were bandaged up:
to see how long a new-born lives

deprived of food. I had no choice.
Each day I chewed my bread
and wrapped it in a scrap of cloth
I soaked in soup. A peasant dummy.

With this I fed my child. My God.
The child lost weight
and every day came Mengele.
Soon she had no strength to cry.

She only whimpered, and my milk got up.
I couldn't give her anything.
Except, about the sixth or seventh day,
the syringe of morphium.

Cut slanted like a quill.
And warm from Matza Steinberg's hand.
I can understand ghosts.
How they have to come back.

What it costs to return
through the bricks of a house.
Eyes tight shut.
Weeping, broken skin.

III *Limbo*

A terraced house in Marston Street.
One north-facing, whitewashed room,
with icons and incense and candles.

Unorthodox Russian Orthodox.
We are praying for your after-life:
'a place of light, of verdure, of repose'.

Blackedged damp-proof membrane.
The pillar that I stand behind
supports a builder's r.s.j.

The ordinary world is a wall away,
where the worst will always happen.
As it always happened to you.

Trained to be a bas-relief,
the undertaker's men stick out,
they overact invisibility.

Like your tail at the Bolshoi
after four hours of *Siegfried*.
Tragic yawns. Unmoved to tears.

The bishop's oily, ignorant eulogy
cannot make up for what was unmade:
for the death of your daughter,

which you sometimes sentimentalised;
for that tumour on the brain
that almost killed your wife

before it took away her looks
and, with them, some of your love.
Nothing is perfect. Not even pain.

I close my eyes to everything –
but catch you pouring out a whisky.
As hard in the end

as threading a needle.
In your stockinged feet,
without a tie, one cuff undone.

The broken leather of your belt
almost breaks my heart.
Whisky and *Weltschmerz*

and whisky, brooding
on the death from cancer
of your closest friend at 54,

while you outlived TB and typhus,
the loss of a lung,
and the time of your life.

Still knowing who you were,
you ceased to be yourself.
And this is after all the after-life.

Liver-coloured lips
await us in the mirror,
glands will cobble our armpits

and the sphygmometer
will pant like a puppy
tightening its leash.

You taught me this.
In bed like a baboon
with your oxygen mask,

tasting the taste of your lung,
dreading the whump of gas,
a coffin charred to astrakhan,

and choosing the grave instead,
this grave your grandson considers
coldly like a conundrum at chess,

the vivid loose covers,
soil swept under the carpet,
the protruding spade.

And this sorrow like salts
seeping slowly out of the plaster.
Crystals slowly coming clear.

IV *Shaman*

I imagined a monster,
flowering envy, the Judas tree
and all the obvious sins,

faeces and faces under wet leaves,
a self of bracken and bodies,
the mind on the trail

of the murdering mind
that masturbates with everything.
And then I found the oracle:

a set of false teeth
like a long-lost tiara
singing in their Steradent.

Honesty shook its tambourines
and I entered the cerebral maze
in search of myself.

Memories of memories of memories:
fainting after my first communion;
Father Watson like the Abbé Liszt,

blu-tacked boldly with cysts
all over his sorrowful face,
saying, You can leave the Church,

but the Church will never leave you.
On the back of my hand,
a rosary of beaded blood.

The roquefort marble of the font
was a match for his teeth.
His soutane was bleached

by an ebb-tide of salts
where it caught him under the arms,
his fingers fine but sulphurous

with Senior Service, forty a day,
kept in a silver case
he consulted like a breviary,

as I faltered on Father,
suddenly struck by the word
which fainted in my fasting mouth.

I was lost in the labyrinth.
Language waited to speak
and then I was home in my head,

hearing the sound of Javanese,
catching the cadence
of everyinthay ackwardsbay.

Long forgotten fluency, practised
in the prefab's living room
of imitation panelled oak,

whose anaglypta walls were painted
bowel-brown with wood-effects.
The windows wept with condensation.

I sat in my cowboy suit,
sewn from sacks on the treadle machine,
listening to lives,

seeing my mother at the cemetery
where she buried her daughter
and remembered a rat.

Past events were visited
until I knew them all by heart,
clear as the kiss curls

she fashioned with spit,
one at each ear.
I could see my dead sister,

dead before I was born:
her tongue like a tinned strawberry,
her baby hair a fingerprint.

I heard the names of houses:
17 Charles Street, Railway Terrace . . .
The great historical seats.

Sitting in my cowboy suit,
I was only my mother,
a girl with thin arms

who slipped with an iron saucepan
and scalded her brother.
His back was damascened with scars,

and she was never forgiven
by the father she loved,
a long time ago in Beresford Street.

I am only my mother
in love with a white summer dress
with fancy buttons at the side

and pansies worked into the wool,
which went with her basket-weave shoes.
The sequins shone in our eyes.

And I am something else.
It was Siberia outside,
the frost was like an undercoat.

The stove with mica panes
was doubled in my father's stare.
He drummed on the sofa arm

and yodelled with the wireless on.
He had returned from the dead
with the gift of tongues:

he spoke to the dark
beyond the bedroom walls,
rapid as a Polish auctioneer,

and the dog would wake
with anxious anapaests,
howling like the dead.

I am only my father,
the healer with head wounds,
who takes on pains in his sleep.

This is the sacred monster,
the sound at the centre,
who is only my father,

irritating, unimportant, vital,
the prophet in a Burton suit,
who knows that his myth

will survive with the maze.
I am only my father
having a fit on the floor,

leaving the body behind
arched in a perfect crab,
while gravity stretches my face

and I hurtle to heaven.

v *Paradise*

It was pure. There was only one snow.
Cuttlefish bones for drift after drift.
I could not feel. My body was gone.
The sky was clear and the wind was white.

It was pure. Except for the plankton
adrift in my eyes, I could have been dead.
My body was gone. There was only one snow.
Of cuttlefish bones alive in the light.

The wind was white. It was aerodynamic.
The wind was like a principle.
It was a force at work on the bones.
And I said no to the wind.

Your thigh is Japanese paper.
The veins are broken threads of mulberry.
By now they exist in my eyes
like a specimen slide.

So I said no to the wind.

VI *A Chest of Drawers*

Out of oblivion, birds,
the heron arranging its shawls,
the tick of a blackbird,
there, like a Chinese spoon,
gulls in gutta-percha overshoes,
and then the sound of the sea
getting out of the bath.

In the big bedroom,
my friend's mother is dying
in front of the children,
her hair like ash,
fragile on the pillowcase.

Out of oblivion, this,
philosophers, fandango dancers,
a Russian-speaking budgerigar,
the torch inside a television,
form and refusal of form,
the thalidomide seal, God,
and the perspex shrimp.

Out at Bellaghy,
my friend's mother is dying,
a clear varnish
of sweat on her face.
Wedding ring tilted and loose.

Out of oblivion, dogs,
the blotting paper pedigree
spattered with Indian ink
and the smoke-ringed poodle,
a pug like a car-crash,
this velvet dachshund's
miniature Madame Récamier.

The young priest is praying,
in a hurry, on his knees
beside an empty cup and saucer.
But the look in her eyes
is cornered, distant, desolate.

Out of oblivion, jazz,
the sea-horse saxophones,
a trumpeter's face, closed,
on the edge of an orgasm,
the tinnitus of cymbals touched,
and then the thought of Lazarus
come back to life with fizzy fingers.

In the big bedroom,
remember phoning the doctor
all those different times ago?
The clammy kiosk
and the damp directory.

Out of oblivion, books,
and Bellow's fabulous freestyle,
the fluid use of *he* and *I*
for outer action and inner life,
adapted from Joyce (a nod
in the name of Moses Herzog)
but made his own by memories.

Come down to the kitchen
and the worn, familiar caddy.
Once you couldn't reach it,
a little boy on a chair
and easily moved.

Out of oblivion, increase,
lobes of labia, wrinkled,
sticky, like an Izmir fig,
a stub of umbilicus
the colours of birdshit,
the shade of ground glass
in a naked glans.

In the big bedroom,
out at Bellaghy,
something always known,
but kept a secret from yourself
because it can't be helped.

Out of oblivion, life,
life and the ineffable skull
which feeds at the breast.
See the spray of milk,
engraving the air,
or standing in stitches,
threads on the thread of the nipple.

Why jazz? Why birds? Why books?
These thousand things are ours
without making sense,
until tomorrow or the next day
or the day after that.

Out of oblivion, death,
and the gaze of a mother's mouth
looking beyond us forever.
Out of oblivion, breath,
and the absence of breath,
the long look we lived in
fixed at last on a chest of drawers.

VII *Coda*

Just before you die,
you are given the sun

and all your mistakes.
Then they are taken away.

Sopot

somewhere

breathless with anxiety
a steam train

swans   swans persist
in the poisoned sea

as the Grand Hotel
persists

the menu's blueprint

brought by the waiter
elytra centre-parted
over his crumpled shirttails

at the end
of the longest wooden pier
in Europe

an aviary

of binoculars
bolted to the balustrade
looks out to sea

persists

Eine kleine Prosa

With wine and cigarettes, we have solved a question. The prose poem can be unpoetic – just anything too short to be a short short story.

What the Germans call *eine kleine Prosa*.

For example. At the outdoor swimming pool, my son, who is eleven, is greeted by a smaller boy, who grins, 'Hello, Isaac, it's me, only I don't have any hair.'

All afternoon the two play games. And Isaac controls the trouble in his voice.

A little boy who doesn't need to wear a bathing hat.

The younger brother of a girl in Isaac's class at school.

Eine kleine Prosa.

Scrap

Starved
on turnip tops
on onion skins   potato peelings

the second River War
had stopped

(and the third
had not begun)

Past the only petrol pump
in Jam Jar City

pushing a KFA
with a broken belt

this dealer in scrap
was heading for home
heading for home

The pump held
a gun to its head
an empty
theatrical gesture

a seagull
blew on a blade of grass

He
was making a song

for his wife
happy   loving   foolish
heading for home

He had only finished
one verse
when he came to the orchard

(beyond it the house)

and propped the KFA
beside a bicycle   asleep
in its cobwebs
in its oxygen tent

and other dim machinery
machinery

the baby
would have been a boy
he saw

he saw at once

when he saw
she was dead

the foetus   unearthed
slateblue face carved
carved hands
between her legs

tiny waistcoat of ribs

on the bloody
divan

     He straightened
the rug

and turned his
head from
side to side to side to
side   like a baby

grazed
by a nipple

hungry
he had finished one verse

turbot move like magic carpets
undulating at a lick
caterpillars move by peristalsis
jellyfish
        by being sick

heading for home

Heaven on Earth

Now that it is night,
you fetch in the washing
from outer space,

from the frozen garden
filmed like a kidney,
with a ghost in your mouth,

and everything you hold,
two floating shirts, a sheet,
ignores the law of gravity.

Only this morning,
the wren at her millinery,
making a baby's soft bonnet,

as we stopped by the spring,
watching the water
well up in the grass,

as if the world were teething.
It was heaven on earth
and it was only the morning.

Shut

The river chemical with fog

a few uncertain
stars   the electricity
undependable   wavering off
and on

Inside the bungalow
by her bed
the king of Pity Me

balancing
beef jelly on
a spoon

a precious uncut stone
wobbling
nervous   upset

her lips pull   slowly
open   the grey stained teeth
decided   shut against the jelly

they cannot change their mind
their mind is shut

a long long long way off

the unpronounceable
stumble and clish

of the spoon   thwarted
alloy   striking the teeth

like a key   a key
key   like a key
in the wrong lock

all consonants

The Bible
open like a wig

The Bible
shut like a rat

and the sounds of confinement
of labour   contraction
of nowhere to go

except into pain

legs   thin-skinned   weepy
shining   solid
damp-stained hands

the pillow a map of saliva
tits tipped with gristle

bald
genitalia   an elephant's eye
wrinkled   shut glint
of moistness

To have known her before
her eyelids alive
laughter   teeth   the tongue
in her mouth   touching the word

subtle   shaping the sounds

Abishag

and the shock of her cunt
like a liqueur chocolate

There is love
in this tottering jelly
irritably offered

brought to those lips
which are shut

then open for good

Muybridge

A dirty   sheet
of contacts

circled
numbered
smeared
of the letter M

the squat of the letter M
taking
her antibiotics

(flesh
disintegrates)

in suppository form
hands   statuesque
in surgical gloves

on the lavatory paper
mortal remains
read like a kidnap demand

knees
drawn up   the letter M
exhausted gorilla arms

defeated by stairs

the hollow
tingle of breath
like anaesthetic

         a dinghy
inflating

but water filling her mouth
flooding her body

the huddle of the letter M

Death Bed

Last things

only three last things
only three live on

a mind
which is carefully losing its mind
reiterates

who wrote *Alice in Wonderland*

and the answer fades
as the question forms
and the answer fades

then water from Aladdin's lamp
this feeding cup for invalids
then khaki from the catheter
then khaki from the catheter

the pulse   a scratch
a scratch

whistling like a dynamo
this one wide-open nostril

thought on its thermal
drifts

watching   unseeing
we consider the cog in snowflakes
the squirrel's strobe   effect

the famous   caught by cameras
facing arrow flights at Agincourt

unlike these finger joints
phalanges   we photograph
a joiner's bit of beading
set aside for further use

thrift
thrift and this ache

brought back to the bedside
by hearing the wail of wood
prised off an empty packing case

one eye   open
breathing has come to a close

brought back
to our twisted faces
as if our mouths held something horrible

trying not to cry

and then
the soul brushed past
like a wind   taking its time

Cadmus

the skin on his forearms
like the skin on eggcustard

his past   coming and going
a dream in the daze of dying

he is in the Post Office
drinking tea   his children
were drowned   were changed
into gods
a moth was magnetised
to the glass
Halloween pumpkin eyes
elephants slobbering

you have to drink tea
and eat and go to the toilet
carefully   you have to concentrate
you can fall anywhere

in the Post Office

a pupa
of chewing gum under the counter

when his skin begins to change
he begins to leave it behind
pulling his body over his body
over his head

dark   tight tight

he shrugs his shoulders off
the ears are difficult

unrecognisable
his aura of cling film
stuck to the carpet tiles

he feels

slim   tight as a woven whip
quilted   bead embroidery
new Missoni knitwear
beautiful again

upper set broken in two
his unintelligible lisp

when they bring a mirror
to test for breath
he sees a snake

wait
no
mistake
mistake

Retirement
(For Terry and Joanna Kilmartin)

The world is a beautiful woman
we love but have ceased to see,

with whom we must learn to linger
all over again, to prize and to praise

all over again, while there is time,
so much time has been lost.

And so we retire, to watch
a dark-blue, touch-paper sky

spasm with trapped light
like the storm in the Xerox machine,

or, looking away, suddenly see
the golf course powder its face.

She is shy and retiring like us
as we seek to redress

the long neglect of a life,
now there is time at last

to bring her out her playful side,
her secret poetry, her deft translations:

the mudflat's manual of knots,
nœud de soldat, nœud de vache,

the spider's virtuoso harp,
the poached egg like an octopus.

The seasons send her inspiration
to the tiring house of dirt,

where she dons and doffs
her naked disguises:

a field fluffy with pompons of clover,
a strand with three strands of pearls.

A Short Essay on the Light Bulb

Moses Farmer   Edison   Irving Langmuir
then the thing itself   naked

as if invention broke

(it should have shone   forever
like the old chipped stars)

naked   but not quite human
a different kind   of nakedness
the truth   and nothing else

which brings us
to this woman   and her side effects
the way her blazing head

is tilted like a lampshade
in the open air

(after surgery
neck   half an ear
a course of radium)

she is bright
and brave and beaten

she has her shopping still to do

and holds her head   so tenderly
she might be taking care of it

for someone else

or   dark

(the wind
the wind is in her wound)

and waiting   waiting   waiting

for illumination

Perfume

She left behind
a fragrant ghost:

the idea of down
on the ear lobes,

a naked wrist,
another wrist,

caressing each other
like delicate lovers,

and scent the shape
of her collar bones,

leaving the air
alive with herself.

Muse

Luck   To have lived
at the level of floorboards
and not to give   a toss

about Antaeus
or any   of that

Only the pleasing precision
of solid dirt
inlaying   the planks

like a long leather bootlace

or finding   the perfect fit
of thumb   to the palate

Carefully torn
wallpaper   sufficient
unto the hour

A mouth
I taste   everything
because I have   no taste

It is enough   this ignorance
these particulars
I kiss

The nails
surrender   a patient light
underlings

their living daylights
a kind of dusk
or sunk   out of sight

like that blackhead   I prize
beside your eyebrow
deep   as your pierced ear

that tag on your neck
like a Coco Pop   scratchy

the white appendix scar
its warp   in the weft
like perished elastic

the linked Assyrian mail
the lair on your private parts

I am too deep   in detail
too deep   to divine
your identity

Urania
Clio
Calliope

or catch all that stuff
you keep singing   about sunsets

Listen   Just listen

Like Santa Claus
the milkman   leaves a xylophone
he walks   down the gravel drive

listen   just listen
like someone eating

eating
sugared almonds

On My Fiftieth Birthday

Is heaven the smell of ironing?
I have come back home.

I have come back home to the body,
to a threadbare tapestry of rain.

There is new grass in the garden,
brittle chemical crystals.

Will I flourish with leaves?
Warts are budding everywhere.

There is a growth on my knee
like a Jerusalem artichoke,

jointed stem ginger.
Where have I been these last ten years?

There is an oar from Cuppers
which props up the clothes-line.

And my heart is Odysseus,
shriven, at the shrine to Poseidon.

War and peace. *War and Peace.*
A cricket ball like Saturn in the undergrowth.

Change

A Victorian girl
pink   plump   in her drawers
like a Christmas cracker

about to lose weight
by eating

a segment of tapeworm
plump
as a cushion of cold ravioli

swallowed
like change

like Mr Patel
a century later
whose life has changed

whose wife has died
who noticed a lump in her breast
on the 16th

the surgeon operated
on the 19th

she was dead
on the 20th

he writes each date
on the Post Office blotter
and circles it

sudden

he shakes his head
unable to speak
unable

swallows

stabs my postal order twice

Watching from the Wings

Outside the dressing rooms,
corporal punishment:
spanking new shoes
on the naughty stone steps.

We have been to the ballet,
exploring back stage:
taking in tights
as tight as a Durex,

stiff little tutus
cut like an Eton crop,
beauty spots of filth
on the dancers' points,

the trembling curve
of well-trained ankles.
Appliqué smiles,
rib-cages stilled,

curtseys, then bows,
and that whiplash of rain
stinging the stage
at curtain call.

Redmond's Hare

Tender as an osteopath,
I turned the stiff neck
to study the four long teeth
clenched like a mortise lock

and took in the dirty blur
of an eye out of focus,
the tiny windswept acres
of black and gold fur,

the penury of sodden paws.
The ears were glove fingers
squeezed through a wringer.
I jiggled a broken claw,

then felt the hard nipples
like a series of shocks,
simple but incredible,
and I looked out the sex:

female, a little black-eye,
too tender to touch,
which only looked at me
and I was crushed

and had to look away.
So I got her undressed,
stiff as a child in a vest
and wild at the end of the day.

King Gilgamesh

We make up our minds

The Scythians could not damage the small city

But Nineveh went under the plough

And all the children
were taken away, were led by the hand

The clasp of electrodes
and so much mud

It was impossible
We could not imagine a flower

That swimming pool of bluebells
just beyond the gates
of the undamaged city

wherever
it is

whose hospital holds
a single shining thermometer

like the last sword swallower left on earth

For Hans Keller

There will be more of this,
more of this than I had realised
of finding our friends

irrevocably changed,

skewed like Guy Fawkes in a chair
because all the muscles have gone
and talking as if nothing has happened

when nothing has happened.

There will be more of this,
more of coming to crematoria
to learn that a life can come to an end

like a Haydn quartet, without a repeat.

There will be too much and then more of this,
of hearing instruments negotiate with silence,
stating the case with gravitas

and anxious insect antennae.

We stand for the coffin at a word from the usher.
The speaker's hand feels for his pocket,
as his nerves die down

and the nerves take over.

That hand is alive and my feet are alive,
feeling the pinch of expensive new shoes,
and I am moved by being moved

as the coffin crawls to the fire.

Hans, there is still more of this,
more of undertakers locking the hearse
and seeing the plastic safety bolts

slide, like suppositories, slowly away,

as we re-enter the sunshine alive
with eyes to see by Camden Lock
a bedstead, sleeping rough,

like dead beloved bodies everywhere.

Notes

The Prophetic Book

Nearly all of 'Sheol' is taken, more or less verbatim, from the testimony of Ruth Elias, a survivor of Dr Josef Mengele's Birkenau and a courageous participant in the mock-trial at Jerusalem during the early months of 1985, when the search for Mengele seemed likely to be successful. I happened to hear her account on the BBC's 'International Assignment', one morning after the 10 o'clock news, and I could not forget it.

For 'Shaman', I consulted various studies which I cannot now precisely recall but which happened to be on the shelves of the anthropological section in Blackwells bookshop in Oxford. My note-books record odds and ends in a completely unscholarly fashion, and it has been an odd experience trying to reconstruct my sources in order to write these notes – with little more to go on than the poem itself. Like any other critic, in fact.

The standard work is *Shamanism: Archaic Techniques of Ecstasy* by Mircea Eliade. I glanced at *Structural Anthropology* by Claude Lévi-Strauss and *Shaman: The Wounded Healer* by Joan Halifax.

The subject is a complex one but here are some quotations which will provide a rudimentary guide.

Shamanism in the strict sense is pre-eminently a religious phenomenon of Siberia and Central Asia. The word comes to us, through the Russian, from the Tungusic *šaman* (Eliade).

Magic and magicians are to be found more or less all over the world, whereas shamanism exhibits a particular magical specialty, on which we shall later dwell at length: 'mastery over fire', 'magical flight', and so on (Eliade).

According to another Yakut account, the evil spirits carry the future shaman's soul to the underworld ... Here the shaman undergoes his initiation. The spirits cut off his head, which they set aside (for the candidate must watch his dismemberment with his own eyes), and cut him into small pieces, which are then distributed to the spirits of the various diseases. Only by undergoing such an ordeal will the future shaman gain the power to cure (Eliade).

In the course of his initiation the future shaman has to learn the secret language that he will use during his seances to communicate with the spirits and animal spirits (Eliade).

In the Arctic the shamanic ecstasy is a spontaneous and organic phenomenon; and it is only in this zone that one can properly speak of a great shamanising, that is, of the ceremony that ends with a real cataleptic trance, during which the soul is supposed to have left the body and to be journeying in the sky or the underworld (Eliade).

The shaman does not limit himself to reproducing or miming certain events. He actually relives them in all their vividness, originality and violence. And since he returns to his normal state at the end of the seance, we may say, borrowing a key term from psychoanalysis, that he *abreacts*. In psychoanalysis, abreaction refers to the decisive moment in the treatment when the patient intensively relives the initial situation from which his disturbance stems, before he ultimately overcomes it. In this sense, the shaman is a professional abreactor.

(Lévi-Strauss, 'The Sorcerer and His Magic')

'Javanese': This way of talking has many names, but I have taken that used by the Goncourt brothers in their journal to describe the way prostitutes talked to each other in front of their clients. Apparently, this argot was borrowed from schoolgirls, and the Goncourts report that it created 'the effect of a stiff brush scouring one's ears'.

Cadmus

An imitation of Ovid's *Metamorphoses*, Book IV, 563–603.

Cadmus, son of Agenor, did not know that his daughter and his little grandson had been transformed into gods of the sea. Overwhelmed with grief at his series of misfortunes, and daunted by the many portents he had seen, the founder departed from his city, as if it were the fortune of the place and not his own which was oppressing him. After long wanderings he and his wife, who had accompanied him in his flight, came to the land of Illyria. Both bowed down now with age and sorrow, they were recalling the early fortunes of their house, and as they talked they reviewed their sufferings. 'Surely,' said Cadmus, 'that must have been a holy snake I slew, the one whose teeth I scattered over the soil as a new kind of seed, long ago in the days when I first left Sidon. If it is his death which the gods are avenging with such unerring anger, I pray that I myself may become a serpent, that my body may be stretched out into that of a long-bellied snake.' As he was speaking, his body did indeed begin to stretch into the long belly of a snake; his skin hardened, and turned black in colour, and he felt scales forming on it, while blue-green spots appeared, to brighten its sombre hue. Then he fell forward on his chest, and his legs, united into one, were gradually thinned away into a smooth pointed tail. His arms yet remained: so holding out these remaining arms, with tears streaming down his still human cheeks: 'Come, my wife, my most unhappy wife,' he said. 'Come, and while something of me yet remains, touch me: take my hand, while it is a hand, before I am entirely changed into a snake.' He tried to say more, but suddenly his tongue divided into two parts – though he wished to speak, words failed him: whenever he made an attempt to lament his fate, he hissed. That was all the voice that Nature left him.

His wife beat her hands against her naked breast. 'Cadmus,' she cried, 'stay, my unhappy Cadmus, rid yourself of this monstrous shape! Cadmus, what is happening? Where are your feet, your hands and shoulders, your fair complexion, your features? – All that is you is vanishing as I speak. You heavenly powers, will you not turn me also into the same kind of snake?' Such were her words. He husband licked her cheeks, and slipped into his wife's bosom, as if into a familiar resting place, embracing and twining himself about the neck he knew so well. All who were there – for their friends were with them – were terrified: but his wife stroked the glistening neck of the crested snake, and suddenly there were two of them, gliding along with coils intertwined, till they disappeared into the shelter of a neighbouring grove. Even now they are friendly snakes, and do not shun mankind, or do them harm, for they remember their former state.

(translation by Mary M. Innes, Penguin Classics, 1955)

Acknowledgements

'The Prophetic Book' was published in a limited edition by Correspondance des Arts, Łódź, in 1988, with a Polish translation by Jerzy Jarniewicz. The sequence was broadcast on BBC Radio 3 with Alan Bennett, Stephanie Cole and Isaac Raine. The producer was Judith Bumpus.

'Change' was published in a limited edition by Prospero Poets, with illustrations by George Hardie.

'Muybridge' was specially commissioned for *Hockney's Alphabet* by David Hockney, the proceeds of which went to the AIDS Crisis Trust.

'On My Fiftieth Birthday' was published in a Festschrift for Ted Hughes's sixty-fifth birthday, *A Parcel of Poems*.

Acknowledgements are also due to the editors of the following: *After Ovid*, *Australian Verse*, *Between Comets*, *Grand Street*, the *Guardian*, the *Independent on Sunday*, *Jacaranda Review*, *Landfall*, the *Listener*, the *London Review of Books*, *New Directions 53* and *54*, *New Writing*, the *New Yorker*, the *Observer*, the *Partisan Review*, *Pivot*, *Ploughshares*, *Poetry Book Society Supplement*, the *Sunday Times*, *Thames Poetry*, *The Times Literary Supplement*, and the *Yale Review*.